Buddhism
in a Nutshell

BY

NĀRADA THERA

Buddhist Publication Society
P.O. Box 61
54, Sangharaja Mawatha
Kandy, Sri Lanka
http://www.bps.lk

First printed: 1982
Reprinted: 2010

National Library of Sri Lanka—
Cataloguing in Publication Data

Narada Thera

Buddhism in a Nutshell / Narada Thera.- Kandy :
Buddhist Publication Society, 2010
BP 106S.- 90p.; 18.5cm

ISBN 978-955-24-0352-1   Price:

i. 294.3 DDC 22   ii. Title
01. Buddhism

ISBN 978-955-24-0352-1

Printed by
Creative Printers & Designers
Bahirawakanda, Kandy.

PREFACE

Buddhism in a Nutshell first appeared in 1933. Since then several editions were published by various philanthropic gentlemen for free distribution.

This new edition has been greatly modified and slightly enlarged.

For a fuller exposition of the subject readers are kindly requested to read the revised and enlarged edition of *The Buddha and His Teachings* published in 1980.

Permission may freely be obtained to reprint or to translate this book.

Nārada Vajirarama,
Colombo

CONTENT

BUDDHISM IN A NUTSHELL

"Namo Tassa Bhagavato Arahanto
Sammā-Sambuddhassa"

THE BUDDHA

On the full moon day of May, in the year 623 B.C.
there was born in the district of Nepal an Indian
Sakya Prince named Siddhattha Gotama, who was
destined to be the greatest religious teacher in the
world. Brought up in the lap of luxury, receiving an
education befitting a prince, human as he was, he
married and had a son.

His contemplative nature and boundless
compassion did not permit him to enjoy the fleeting
material pleasures of a Royal household. He knew no
woe, but he felt a deep pity for sorrowing humanity.
Amidst comfort and prosperity, he realized the
universality of sorrow. The palace, with all its worldly
amusements, was no longer a congenial place for the
compassionate prince. The time was ripe for him to
depart. Realizing the vanity of sensual enjoyments, in
his twenty-ninth year, he renounced all worldly
pleasures and donning the simple yellow garb of an
ascetic, alone, penniless, wandered forth in search of
Truth and Peace.

It was an unprecedented historic renunciation;
for he renounced not in his old age but in the prime
of manhood, not in poverty but in plenty. As it was
the belief in the ancient days that no deliverance
could be gained unless one leads a

3

life of strict asceticism, he strenuously practised all forms of severe austerities. "Adding vigil after vigil, and penance after penance," he made a superhuman effort for six long years.

His body was reduced to almost a skeleton. The more he tormented his body, the farther his goal receded from him. The painful, unsuccessful austerities which he strenuously practised proved absolutely futile. He was now fully convinced, through personal experience, of the utter futility of self-mortification which weakened his body and resulted in lassitude of spirit.

Benefiting by this invaluable experience of his, he finally decided to follow an independent course, avoiding the two extremes of self-indulgence and self-mortification. The former retards one's spiritual progress, and the latter weakens one's intellect. The new way which he himself discovered was the Middle Path, *majjhima paṭipadā*, which subsequently became one of the salient characteristics of his teaching.

One happy morning, while he was deeply absorbed in meditation, unaided and unguided by any supernatural power and solely relying on his efforts and wisdom, he eradicated all defilements, purified himself, and, realizing things as they truly are, attained Enlightenment (Buddhahood) at the ripe age of 35. He was not born a Buddha,[1] but he became

---

1.   An Awakened or Enlightened One.

a Buddha by his own striving. As the perfect embodiment of all the virtues he preached, endowed with deep wisdom commensurate with his boundless compassion, he devoted the remainder of his precious life to serve humanity both by example and precept, dominated by no personal motive whatever.

After a very successful ministry of 45 long years the Buddha, as every other human being, succumbed to the inexorable law of change, and finally passed away in his 80th year, exhorting his disciples to regard his doctrine as their teacher.

The Buddha was a human being. As a man he was born, as a man he lived, and as a man his life came to an end. Though a human being, he became an extraordinary man (*acchariya manussa*), but he never arrogated to himself divinity. The Buddha laid stress on this important point and left no room whatever for anyone to fall into the error of thinking that he was an immortal divine being. Fortunately there is no deification in the case of the Buddha. It should, however, be remarked that there was no Teacher "ever so godless as the Buddha, yet none so god-like."

The Buddha is neither an incarnation of the Hindu God Vishnu, as is believed by some, nor is he a savior who freely saves others by his personal salvation. The Buddha exhorts his disciples to depend on themselves for their deliverance, for both purity and defilement depend on oneself. Clarifying his relationship with his followers and emphasizing the importance of self-reliance and individual striving, the Buddha plainly states: "You should exert yourselves, the Tathāgatas[2] are only teachers."

The Buddhas point out the path, and it is left for us to follow that path to obtain our purification.

"To depend on others for salvation is negative, but to depend on oneself is positive." Dependence on others means a surrender of one's effort.

In exhorting his disciples to be self-dependent the Buddha says in the *Parinibbāna Sutta*: "Be islands unto yourselves, be a refuge unto yourselves, seek not for refuge in others." These significant words are self-elevating. They reveal how vital is self-exertion to accomplish one's object and, how superficial and futile is to seek redemption through benignant saviours and to crave for illusory happiness in an after-life through the propitiation of imaginary gods or by irresponsive prayers and meaningless sacrifices.

Furthermore, the Buddha does not claim the monopoly of Buddhahood which, as a matter of fact, is not the prerogative of any specially graced person. He reached the highest possible state of perfection any person could aspire to, and without the close-fist of a teacher he revealed the only straight path that leads thereto. According to the Teachings of the Buddha anybody may aspire to that supreme state of perfection if he makes the necessary exertion. The Buddha does not condemn men by calling them

---

2. Lit., Thus who hath come.

wretched sinners, but, on the contrary, he gladdens them by saying that they are pure in heart at conception. In his opinion the world is not wicked,, but is deluded by ignorance. Instead of disheartening his followers and reserving that exalted state only to himself, he encourages and induces them to emulate him, for Buddhahoood is latent in all. In one sense all are potential Buddhas.

One who aspires to become a Buddha is called a Bodhisatta, which, literally, means a wisdom-being. This Bodhisatta ideal is the most beautiful and the most refined course of life that has ever been presented to this ego-centric world, for what is nobler than a life of service and purity?

As a man he attained Buddhahood and proclaimed to the world the latent inconceivable possibilities and the creative power of man. Instead of placing an unseen Almighty God over man who arbitrarily controls the destinies of mankind, and making him subservient to a supreme power, he raised the worth of mankind. It was he who taught that man can gain his deliverance and purification by his own exertion without depending on an external God or mediating priests. It was he who taught the ego-centric world the noble ideal of selfless service. It was he who revolted against the degrading caste system and taught equality of mankind and gave equal opportunities for all to distinguish themselves in every walk of life.

He declared that the gates of success and prosperity were open to all in every condition of life, high or low, saint or criminal, who would care to turn a new leaf and aspire to perfection.

Irrespective of caste, colour or rank he established for both deserving men and women a democratically constituted celibate Order. He did not force his followers to be slaves either to his Teachings or to himself but granted complete freedom of thought.

He comforted the bereaved by his consoling words. He ministered to the sick that were deserted. He helped the poor that were neglected. He ennobled the lives of the deluded, purified the corrupted lives of criminals. He encouraged the feeble, united the divided, enlightened the ignorant, clarified the mystic, guided the benighted, elevated the base, dignified the noble. Both rich and poor, saints and criminals loved him alike. Despotic and righteous kings, famous and obscure princes and nobles, generous and stingy millionaires, haughty and humble scholars, destitute paupers, down-trodden scavengers, wicked murderers, despised courtesans— all benefited by his words of wisdom and compassion.

His noble example was a source of inspiration to all. His serene and peaceful countenance was a soothing sight to the pious eyes. His message of Peace and Tolerance was welcomed by all with indescribable joy and was of eternal benefit to every one who had the fortune to hear and practise it. Wherever his teaching penetrated it left an indelible impression upon the character of the respective peoples. The cultural advancement of all the Buddhist nations was mainly due to his sublime Teachings. In fact all Buddhist countries like Ceylon, Burma, Thailand, Cambodia, Vietnam, Laos, Nepal, Tibet, China, Mongolia, Korea, Japan, etc., grew up in the cradle of Buddhism. Though more than 2500 years have elapsed since the passing away of this greatest Teacher, yet his unique personality exerts a great influence on all who come to know him.

His iron-will, profound wisdom, universal love, boundless compassion, selfless service, historic renunciation, perfect purity, magnetic personality, exemplary methods employed to propagate the Teachings, and his final success—all these factors have compelled about one-fifth of the population of the world today to hail the Buddha as their supreme religious Teacher.

Paying a glowing tribute to the Buddha Sri Radhakrishna states: "In Gautama the Buddha we have a master-mind from the East second to none so far as the influence on the thought and life of the human race is concerned, and, sacred to all as the founder of a religious tradition whose hold is hardly less wide and deep than any other. He belongs to the history of the world's thought, to the general inheritance of all cultivated men, for, judged by intellectual integrity, moral earnestness, and spiritual insight, he is undoubtedly one of the greatest figures in history."

In *The Three Greatest Men* in History H. G. Wells writes:

"In the Buddha you see clearly a man, simple, devout, lonely, battling for light—a vivid human personality, not a myth. He too gave a message to mankind universal in character.

Many of our best modern ideas are in closest harmony with it. All the miseries and discontents are due, he taught, to selfishness. Before a man can become serene he must cease to live for his senses or himself: Then he merges into a great being Buddha in different language called men to self-forgetfulness 500 years before Christ. In some ways he is nearer to us and our needs. He was more lucid upon our individual importance and service than Christ and less ambiguous upon the question of personal immortality."

St. Hilaire remarks "The perfect model of all the virtues he preaches … His life has not a stain upon it":

Fausböll says "The more I know him, the more I love him."

A humble follower of his would say—"The more I know him, the more I love him; the more I love him, the more I know him."

Chapter 2

THE DHAMMA

Is it a Philosophy?

The non-aggressive, moral and philosophical system expounded by the Buddha, which demands no blind faith from its adherents, expounds no dogmatic creeds, encourages no superstitious rites and ceremonies, but advocates a golden mean that guides a disciple through pure living and pure thinking to the gain of supreme wisdom and deliverance from all evil, is called the Dhamma and is popularly known as Buddhism.

The all-merciful Buddha has passed away, but the sublime Dhamma which He unreservedly bequeathed to humanity, still exists in its pristine purity.

Although the Master has left no written records of his Teachings, his distinguished disciples preserved them by committing to memory and transmitting them orally from generation to generation.

Immediately after his demise 500 chief Arahants[3] versed in the Dhamma[4] and Vinaya,[5] held

---

3. Literally, the Worthy Ones. They are the enlightened disciples who have destroyed all passions.

a convocation to rehearse the Doctrine as was originally taught by the Buddha. Venerable

Ānanda Thera, who enjoyed the special privilege of hearing all the discourses, recited the Dhamma, while the Venerable Upāli recited the Vinaya.

The *Tipiṭaka* was compiled and arranged in its present form by those Arahants of old.

During the reign of the pious Sinhala King Vaṭṭagāmaṇi Abhaya, about 83 B.C., the Tipiṭaka was, for the first time in the history of Buddhism, committed to writing on ola palm leaves in Ceylon.

This voluminous *Tipiṭaka*, which contains the essence of the Buddha's Teaching, is estimated to be about eleven times the size of the Bible. A striking contrast between the Tipiṭaka and the Bible is that the former is not a gradual development like the latter.

As the word itself implies the *Tipiṭaka* consists of three baskets. They are the Basket of Discipline (*Vinaya Piṭaka*), the Basket of Discourses (*Sutta Piṭaka*), and the Basket of Ultimate Doctrine (*Abhidhamma Piṭaka*).

The *Vinaya Piṭaka* which is regarded as the sheet anchor of the oldest historic celibate order—the Saṅgha—mainly deals with rules and regulations which the Buddha promulgated, as occasion arose, for the future discipline of the Order of monks

---

4.   The Teaching
5.   The Discipline

(*Bhikkhus*) and nuns (*Bhikkhunīs*). It describes in detail the gradual development of the *Sāsana* (Dispensation). An account of the life and ministry of the Buddha is also given. Indirectly it reveals some important and interesting information about ancient history, Indian customs, arts, science, etc.

This Piṭaka consists of the five following books:

1. *Pārājika Pāḷi*—Major Offences
2. *Pācittiya Pāḷi*—Minor Offences, Vibhaṅga
3. *Mahāvagga Pāḷi*—Greater Section, Khandaka
4. *Cullavagga Pāḷi*—Shorter Section
5. *Parivāra Pāḷi*—Epitome of the Vinaya

The *Sutta Piṭaka* consists chiefly of discourses, delivered by the Buddha himself on various occasions. There are also a few discourses delivered by some of his distinguished disciples such as the Venerable Sāriputta, Ānanda, Moggallāna, etc., included in it. It is like a book of prescriptions, as the sermons embodied therein were expounded to suit the different occasions and the temperaments of various persons. There may be seemingly contradictory statements, but they should not be misconstrued as they were opportunely uttered by the Buddha to suit a particular purpose: for instance, to the selfsame question he would maintain silence (when the inquirer is merely foolishly inquisitive), or give a detailed reply when he knew the inquirer to be an earnest seeker. Most of the sermons were intended mainly for the benefit of Bhikkhus and they deal with the Holy life and with the exposition of the doctrine. There are also several other discourses which deal with both the material and moral progress of his lay followers.

This Piṭaka is divided into five Nikāyas or collections, viz:

1. *Dīgha Nikāya* (Collection of Long Discourses),
2. *Majjhima Nikāya* (Collection of Middle-length Discourses),
3. *Saṃyutta Nikāya* (Collection of Connected Discourses Sayings),
4. *Aṅguttara Nikāya* (Collection of Gradual Discourses, arranged in accordance with numbers),
5. *Khuddaka Nikāya* (Smaller Collection).

The fifth is subdivided into fifteen books:

1. *Khuddakapāṭha* (Shorter Texts),
2. *Dhammapada* (Way of Truth),
3. *Udāna* (Paeans of Joy),
4. *Itivuttaka* ("Thus said" Discourses),
5. *Suttanipāta* (Group of Discourses),
6. *Vimānavatthu* (Stories of Celestial Mansions),
7. *Petavatthu* (Stories of Departed Ones),
8. *Theragāthā* (Verses of the Senior Monks),
9. *Therigātha* (Verses of the Senior Nuns),
10. *Jātaka* (Birth Stories),
11. *Niddesa* (Expositions),
12. *Paṭisambhidā* (Analytical Knowledge),
13. *Apadāna* (Lives of Arahants),

14. *Buddhavaṃsa* (The Chronicle of Buddhas),
15. *Cariyāpiṭaka* (Modes of Conduct).

The *Abhidhamma Piṭaka* is the most interesting of the three, containing as it does the profound philosophy of the Buddha's Teaching in contrast to the illuminating and simpler discourses in the Sutta Piṭaka.

In the *Sutta Piṭaka* is found the conventional teaching (*vohāra-desanā*) while in the *Abhidhamma Piṭaka* is found the ultimate teaching (*paramattha-desanā*).

To the wise, Abhidhamma is an indispensable guide; to the spiritually evolved, an intellectual treat; and to research scholars, food for thought. Consciousness is defined. Thoughts are analysed and classified chiefly from an ethical standpoint. Mental states are enumerated. The composition of each type of consciousness is set forth in detail. How thoughts arise, is minutely described. Irrelevant problems that interest mankind but having no relation to one's purification, are deliberately set aside.

Matter is summarily discussed; fundamental units of matter, properties of matter, sources of matter, relationship between mind and matter, are explained.

The Abhidhamma investigates mind and matter, the two composite factors of the so-called being, to help the understanding of things as they truly are, and a philosophy has been developed on those lines.

Based on that philosophy, an ethical system has been evolved, to realize the ultimate goal, Nibbāna.

The *Abhidhamma Piṭaka* consists of seven books:

1. *Dhammasaṅgaṇī* (Classification of Dhammas),
2. *Vibhaṅga* (The Book of Divisions),
3. *Kathā Vatthu* (Points of Controversy),
4. *Puggala Paññatti* (Description of Individuals),
5. *Dhātu Kathā* (Discussion with reference to elements)
6. *Yamaka* (The Book of Pairs),
7. *Paṭṭhāna (The Book of Relations)*

In the Tipiṭaka one finds milk for the babe and meat for the strong, for the Buddha taught his doctrine both to the masses and to the intelligentsia. The sublime Dhamma enshrined in these sacred texts, deals with truths and facts, and is not concerned with theories and philosophies which may be accepted as profound truths today only to be thrown overboard tomorrow. The Buddha has presented us with no new astounding philosophical theories, nor did he venture to create any new material science. He explained to us what is within and without, so far as it concerns our emancipation, and ultimately expounded a path of deliverance, which is unique. Incidentally, he has, however, forestalled many a modern scientist and philosopher.

Schopenhauer in his *World as Will and Idea* has presented the truth of suffering and its cause in a Western garb. Spinoza, though he denies not the existence of a permanent reality,. asserts that all phenomenal existence is transitory. In his opinion sorrow is conquered "by finding an object of knowledge which is not transient, not ephemeral, but is immutable, permanent, everlasting." Berkeley proved that the so-called indivisible atom is a metaphysical fiction. Hume, after a relentless. analysis of the mind, concluded that consciousness consists of fleeting mental states. Bergson advocates the doctrine of change. Prof. James refers to a stream of consciousness.

The Buddha expounded these doctrines of transiency, (*anicca*) sorrow (*dukkha*), and no-soul (*anattā*) some 2500 years ago while he was sojourning in the valley of the Ganges.

It should be understood that the Buddha did not preach all that he knew. On one occasion while the Buddha was, passing through a forest he took a handful of leaves and said: "O Bhikkhus, what I have taught is comparable to the leaves in my hand. What I have not taught is comparable to the amount of leaves in the forest."

He taught what he deemed was absolutely essential for one's purification making no distinction between an esoteric and exoteric doctrine. He was characteristically silent on questions irrelevant to his noble mission.

Buddhism no doubt accords with science, but both should be treated as parallel teachings, since one deals mainly with material truths while the other confines itself to moral and spiritual truths. The subject matter of each is, different.

The Dhamma he taught is not merely to be preserved in books, nor is it a subject to be studied from an historical or literary standpoint. On the contrary it is to be learnt and put into practice in the course of one's daily life, for without practice one cannot appreciate the truth. The Dhamma is to be studied, and more to be practised, and above all to be realized: immediate realization is its ultimate goal. As such the Dhamma is compared to a raft which is meant for the sole purpose of escaping from the ocean of birth and death (*saṃsāra*).

Buddhism, therefore, cannot strictly be called a mere philosophy because it is not merely the "love of, inducing the search after, wisdom." Buddhism may approximate a philosophy, but it is very much more comprehensive.

Philosophy deals mainly with knowledge and is not concerned with practice; whereas Buddhism lays special emphasis on practice and realization.

Chapter 3

IS BUDDHISM A RELIGION?

It is neither a religion in the sense in which that word is commonly understood, for it is not "a system of faith and worship owing any allegiance to a supernatural being."

Buddhism does not demand blind faith from its adherents. Here mere belief is dethroned and is substituted by confidence based on knowledge, which, in Pali, is known as *saddhā*. The confidence placed by a follower on the Buddha is like that of a sick person in a noted physician, or a student in his teacher. A Buddhist seeks refuge in the Buddha because it was he who discovered the Path of Deliverance.

A Buddhist does not seek refuge in the Buddha with the hope that he will be saved by his personal purification. The Buddha gives no such guarantee. It is not within the power of a Buddha to wash away the impurities of others. One could neither purify nor defile another.

The Buddha, as Teacher, instructs us, but we ourselves are directly responsible for our purification.

Although a Buddhist seeks refuge in the Buddha, he does not make any self-surrender. Nor does a Buddhist sacrifice his freedom of thought by becoming a follower of the Buddha. He can exercise his own free will and develop his knowledge even to the extent of becoming a Buddha himself.

The starting point of Buddhism is reasoning or understanding, or, in other words, *sammā-diṭṭhi*.
To the seekers of truth the Buddha says:

"Do not accept anything on (mere) hearsay—(i.e., thinking that thus have we heard it from a long time). Do not accept anything by mere tradition—(i.e. thinking that it has thus been handed down through many generations). Do not accept anything on account of mere rumours—(i.e. by believing what others say without any investigation). Do not accept anything just because it accords with your scriptures. Do not accept anything by mere supposition. Do not accept anything by mere inference. Do not accept anything by merely considering, the reasons. Do not accept anything merely because it agrees with your pre-conceived notions. Do not accept anything merely because it seems acceptable—(i.e., thinking that as the speaker seems to be a good person his word should be accepted), Do not accept anything thinking that the ascetic is respected by us (therefore it is right to accept his word).

"But when you know for yourselves—these things are immoral, these things are blameworthy, these things are censured by the wise, these things, when performed and undertaken, conduce to ruin and sorrow—then indeed do you reject them.

"When you know for yourselves—these things are moral, these things are blameless, these things are praised by the wise, these things, when performed and undertaken, conduce to well-being and happiness—then do you live acting accordingly."

These inspiring words of the Buddha still retain their original force and freshness.

Though there is no blind faith, one might argue whether there is no worshipping of images etc. in Buddhism.

Buddhists do not worship an image expecting worldly or spiritual favours, but pay their reverence to what it represents.

An understanding Buddhist, in offering flowers and incense to an image, designedly makes himself feel that he is in the presence of the living Buddha and thereby gains inspiration from his noble personality and breathes deep his boundless compassion. He tries to follow his noble example.

The Bo-tree is also a symbol of Enlightenment. These external objects of reverence are not absolutely necessary, but they are useful as they tend to concentrate one's attention. An intellectual person could dispense with them as he could easily focus his attention and visualise the Buddha.

For our own good, and out of gratitude, we pay such external respect but what the Buddha expects from his disciples is not so much obeisance as the actual observance of his Teachings. The Buddha says—"He honours me best who practises my teaching best." "He who sees the Dhamma sees me."

With regard to images, however, Count Kaiserling remarks "I see nothing more grand in this world than the image of the Buddha. It is an absolutely perfect embodiment of spirituality in the visible domain."

Furthermore, it must be mentioned that there are no petitional or intercessory prayers in Buddhism. However much we may pray to the Buddha we cannot be saved. The Buddha does not grant favours to those who pray to him. Instead of petitional prayers there is meditation that leads to self-control, purification and enlightenment. Meditation is neither a silent reverie nor keeping the mind blank. It is an active striving. It serves as a tonic both to the heart and the mind. The Buddha not only speaks of the futility of offering prayers but also disparages a slave mentality. A Buddhist should not pray to be saved, but should rely on himself and win his freedom.

"Prayers take the character of private communications, selfish bargaining with God. It seeks for objects of earthly ambitions and inflames the sense of self. Meditation on the other hand is self-change."[6]

In Buddhism there is not, as in most other religions, an almighty God to be obeyed and feared. The Buddha does not believe in a cosmic potentate, omniscient and omnipresent. In Buddhism there are

---

6. Sri Radhakrishna.

no divine revelations or divine messengers. A Buddhist is, therefore, not subservient to any higher supernatural power which controls his destinies and which arbitrarily rewards and punishes. Since Buddhists do not believe in revelations of a divine being Buddhism does not claim the monopoly of truth and does not condemn any other religion. But Buddhism recognises the infinite latent possibilities of man and teaches that man can gain deliverance from suffering by his own efforts independent of divine help or mediating priests.

Buddhism cannot, therefore, strictly be called a religion because it is neither a system of faith and worship, nor "the outward act or form by which men indicate their recognition of the existence of a God or gods having power over their own destiny to whom obedience, service, and honour are due."

If, by religion, is meant "a teaching which takes a view of life that is more than superficial, a teaching which looks into life and not merely at it, a teaching which furnishes men with a guide to conduct that is in accord with this its in-look, a teaching which enables those who give it heed to face life with fortitude and death with serenity,"[7] or a system to get rid of the ills of life, then it is certainly a religion of religions.

---

7. Bhikkhu Sīlācāra

Chapter 4

IS BUDDHISM AN ETHICAL SYSTEM?

It no doubt contains an excellent ethical code which is unparalleled in its perfection and altruistic attitude. It deals with one way of life for the monks and another for the laity. But Buddhism is much more than an ordinary moral teaching. Morality is only the preliminary stage on the Path of Purity, and is a means to an end, but not an end in itself. Conduct, though essential, is itself insufficient to gain one's emancipation. It should be coupled with wisdom or knowledge (*paññā*). The base of Buddhism is morality, and wisdom is its apex..

In observing the principles of morality a Buddhist should not only regard his own self but also should have a consideration for others as well—animals not excluded. Morality in Buddhism is not founded on any doubtful revelation nor is it the ingenious invention of an exceptional mind, but it is a rational and practical code based on verifiable facts and individual experience.

It should be mentioned that any external supernatural agency plays no part whatever in the moulding of the character of a Buddhist. In Buddhism there is no one to reward or punish. Pain or happiness are the inevitable results of one's actions. The question of incurring the pleasure or displeasure of a God does not enter the mind of a Buddhist. Neither hope of reward nor fear of punishment acts as an incentive to him to do good or to refrain from evil. A Buddhist is aware of future consequences, but he refrains from evil because it retards, does good because it aids, progress to Enlightenment (Bodhi). There are also some who do good because it is good, refrain from evil because it is bad.

To understand the exceptionally high standard of morality the Buddha expects from his ideal followers, one must carefully read the Dhammapada, Sigālovāda Sutta, Vyagghapajja Sutta, Maṅgala Sutta, Karaniya Sutta, Parābhava Sutta, Vasala Sutta, Dhammika Sutta, etc.

As a moral teaching it excels all other ethical systems, but morality is only the beginning and not the end of Buddhism.

In one sense Buddhism is not a philosophy, in another sense it is the philosophy of philosophies.

In one sense Buddhism is not a religion, in another sense it is the religion of religions.

Buddhism is neither a metaphysical path nor a ritualistic path.

It is neither sceptical nor dogmatic.

It is neither self-mortification nor self-indulgence.

It is neither pessimism nor optimism.

It is neither eternalism nor nihilism.

It is neither absolutely this-worldly nor other-worldly.

It is a unique Path of Enlightenment.

The original Pali term for Buddhism is Dhamma, which, literally, means that which upholds. There is no English equivalent that exactly conveys the meaning of the Pali term.

The Dhamma is that which really is. It is the Doctrine of Reality. It is a means of Deliverance from suffering, and Deliverance itself. Whether the Buddhas arise or not the Dhamma exists. It lies hidden from the ignorant eyes of men, till a Buddha, an Enlightened One, realizes and compassionately reveals it to the world.

This Dhamma is not something apart from oneself, but is closely associated with oneself. As such the Buddha exhorts:

"Abide with oneself as an island, with oneself as a Refuge. Abide with the Dhamma as an island, with the Dhamma as a Refuge. Seek no external refuge." (*Parinibbāna Sutta*).

Chapter 5

SOME SALIENT FEATURES OF BUDDHISM

The foundations of Buddhism are the four Noble Truths -namely, Suffering (the *raison d'etre* of Buddhism), its cause, i.e. Craving, its end i.e. Nibbāna, (the Summum Bonum of Buddhism), and the Middle Way.

What is the Noble Truth of Suffering?

"Birth is suffering, old age is suffering, disease is suffering, death is suffering, to be united with the unpleasant is suffering, to be separated from the pleasant is suffering, not to receive what one craves for is suffering, in brief the five Aggregates of Attachment are suffering.

What is the Noble Truth of the Cause of Suffering?

"It is the craving which leads from rebirth to rebirth accompanied by lust of passion, which delights now here now there; it is the craving for sensual pleasures (*Kāmataṇhā*), for existence (*bhavataṇhā*)[8] and for annihilation (*vibhavataṇhā*).[9]

---

8. Craving associated with "Eternalism" (*Sassatadiṭṭhi*) (Comy)
9. Craving associated with "Nihilism" (*ucchedadiṭṭhi*) (Comy)

What is the Noble Truth of the Annihilation of Suffering?

"It is the remainderlessness, total annihilation of this very craving, the forsaking of it, the breaking loose, fleeing, deliverance from it.

What is the Noble Truth of the Path leading to the Annihilation of Suffering?

"It is the Noble Eightfold Path which consists of right understanding, right thoughts, right speech, right action, right livelihood, right endeavour, right mindfulness, and right concentration."

Whether the Buddhas arise or not these four Truths exist in the universe. The Buddhas only reveal these Truths which lay hidden in the dark abyss of time.

Scientifically interpreted, the Dhamma may be called the law of cause and effect. These two embrace the entire body of the. Buddha's Teachings.

The first three represent the philosophy of Buddhism; the fourth represents the ethics of Buddhism, based on that philosophy. All these four truths are dependent on this body itself. The Buddha states: "In this very one-fathom long body along with perceptions and thoughts, do I proclaim the world, the origin of the world, the end of the world and the path leading to the end of the world." Here the term world is applied to suffering.

Buddhism rests on the pivot of sorrow. But it does not thereby follow that Buddhism is pessimistic. It is neither totally pessimistic nor totally optimistic, but, on the contrary, it teaches a truth that lies midway between them. One would be justified in calling the Buddha a pessimist if he had only enunciated the Truth of suffering without suggesting a means to put an end to it. The Buddha perceived the universality of sorrow and did prescribe a panacea for this universal sickness of humanity. The highest conceivable happiness, according to the Buddha, is Nibbāna, which is the total extinction of suffering.

The author of the article on Pessimism in the *Encyclopedia Britannica* writes: "Pessimism denotes an attitude of hopelessness towards life, a vague general opinion that pain and evil predominate in human affairs. The original doctrine of the Buddha is in fact as optimistic as any optimism of the West. To call it pessimism is merely to apply to it a characteristically Western principle to which happiness is impossible without personality. The true Buddhist looks forward with enthusiasm to absorption into eternal bliss."

Ordinarily the enjoyment of sensual pleasures is the highest and only happiness of the average man. There is no doubt a kind of momentary happiness in the anticipation, gratification and retrospection of such fleeting material pleasures, but they are illusive and temporary. According to the Buddha non-attachment is a greater bliss.

The Buddha does not expect his followers to be constantly pondering on suffering and lead a miserable unhappy life. He exhorts them to be always happy and cheerful, for zest (*pīti*) is one of the factors of Enlightenment.

Real happiness is found within, and is not to be defined in terms of wealth, children, honours or fame. If such possessions are misdirected, forcibly or unjustly obtained, misappropriated or even viewed with attachment, they will be a source of pain and sorrow to the possessors.

Instead of trying to rationalise suffering, Buddhism takes suffering for granted and seeks the cause to eradicate it. Suffering exists as long as there is craving. It can only be annihilated by treading the Noble Eightfold Path and attaining the supreme bliss of Nibbāna.

These four Truths can be verified by experience. Hence the Buddha Dhamma is not based on the fear of the unknown, but is founded on the bedrock of facts which can be tested by ourselves and verified by experience. Buddhism is, therefore; rational and intensely practical.

Such a rational and practical system cannot contain mysteries or esoteric doctrines. Blind faith, therefore, is foreign to Buddhism. Where there is no blind faith there cannot be any coercion or persecution or fanaticism. To the unique credit of Buddhism it must be said that throughout its peaceful march of 2500 years no drop of blood was shed in the name of the Buddha, no mighty monarch wielded his powerful sword to propagate the Dhamma, and no conversion was made either by force or by repulsive methods. Yet, the Buddha was the first and the greatest missionary that lived on earth.

Aldous Huxley writes: "Alone of all the great world religions Buddhism made its way without persecution, censorship ,or inquisition."

Lord Russell remarks: "Of the great religions of history, I prefer Buddhism, especially in its earliest forms; because .it has had the smallest element of persecution."

In the name of Buddhism no altar was reddened with the blood of a Hypatia, no Bruno was burnt alive.

Buddhism appeals more to the intellect than to the emotion. It is concerned more with the character of the devotees than ,with their numerical strength.

On one occasion Upāli, a follower of Nigaṇṭha Nātaputta, approached the Buddha and was so pleased with the Buddha's exposition of the Dhamma that he instantly expressed his desire to become a follower of the Buddha. But the Buddha cautioned him, saying:

"Of a verity, O householder, make a thorough investigation. It is well for a distinguished man like you to (first) make a thorough investigation."

Upāli, who was overjoyed at this unexpected remark of the Buddha, said "Lord, had I been a follower of another religion, its adherents would have taken me round the streets in a procession proclaiming that such and such a millionaire had renounced his former faith and embraced theirs. But, Lord, Your Reverence advises me to investigate further. The more pleased am I with this remark of yours. For the second time, Lord, I seek refuge in the Buddha, Dhamma and the Sangha."

Buddhism is saturated with this spirit of free enquiry and complete tolerance. It is the teaching of the open mind and the sympathetic heart, which, lighting and warming the whole universe with its twin rays of wisdom and compassion, sheds its genial glow on every being struggling in the ocean of birth and death.

The Buddha was so tolerant that he did not even exercise his power to give commandments to his lay followers. Instead of using the imperative, he said: "It behoves you to do this—It behoves you not to do this." He commands not but does exhort.

This tolerance the Buddha extended to men, women and all living beings.

It was the Buddha, who first attempted to abolish slavery and vehemently protested against the degrading caste-system which was firmly rooted in the soil of India. In the Word of the Buddha it is not by mere birth one becomes an outcast or a noble, but by one's actions. Caste or colour does not preclude one from becoming a Buddhist or from entering. the Order. Fishermen, scavengers, courtesans, together with warriors and Brahmins, were freely admitted to the Order and enjoyed equal privileges and were also given positions of rank. Upāli, the barber for instance, was made in preference to all others the chief in matters pertaining to Vinaya discipline. The timid Sunīta, the scavenger, who attained Arahantship was admitted by the Buddha himself into the Order. Aṅgulimāla, the robber and criminal, was converted to a compassionate saint. The fierce Āḷavaka sought refuge in the Buddha and became a saint. The courtesan Ambapāli entered the Order and attained Arahantship. Such instances could easily be multiplied from the Tipiṭaka to show that the portals of Buddhism were wide open to all, irrespective of caste, colour or rank.

It was also the Buddha who raised the status of downtrodden women and not only brought them to a realization of their importance to society but also founded the first celibate religious order for women with rules and regulations.

The Buddha did not humiliate women, but only regarded them as feeble by nature. He saw the innate good of both men and women and assigned to them their due places in his teaching. Sex is no barrier to attaining Sainthood.

Sometimes the Pali term used to denote women is "*mātu-gāma*" which means mother-folk or society of mothers. As a mother, woman holds an honourable place in Buddhism. Even the wife is regarded as "the best friend" (*paramā sakhā*) of the husband.

Hasty critics are only making ex parte statements when they reproach Buddhism with being inimical to women. Although at first the

33

Buddha refused to admit women into the Order on reasonable grounds, yet later he yielded to the entreaties of his foster-mother, Pajāpatī Gotamī, and founded the Bhikkhunī Order. Just as the Arahants Sāriputta and Moggallāna were made the two chief disciples in the Order of monks, even so he appointed Arahants Khemā and Uppalavaṇṇā as the two chief female disciples. Many other female disciples too were named by the Buddha himself as his distinguished and pious followers.

On one occasion the Buddha said to King Kosala who was displeased on hearing that a daughter was born to him:"

"A woman child, O Lord of men, may prove
Even a better offspring than a male."

Many women, who otherwise would have fallen into oblivion, distinguished themselves in various ways, and gained their emancipation by following the Dhamma and entering the Order. In this new Order, which later proved to be a great blessing to many women, queens, princesses, daughters of noble families, widows, bereaved mothers, destitute women, pitiable courtesans—all, despite their caste or rank, met on a common platform, enjoyed perfect consolation and peace, and breathed that free atmosphere which is denied to those cloistered in cottages and palatial mansions.

It was also the Buddha who banned the sacrifice of poor beasts and admonished his followers to extend their loving kindness (*mettā*) to all living beings—even to the tiniest creature that crawls at one's feet. No man has the power or the right to destroy the life of another as life is precious to all.

A genuine Buddhist would exercise this loving-kindness towards every living being and identify himself with all, making no distinction whatsoever with regard to caste, colour or sex.

It is this Buddhist *mettā* that attempts to break all the barriers which separate one from another. There is no reason to keep aloof from others merely because they belong to another persuasion or another nationality. In that noble *Toleration Edict* which is based on *Culla-Vyūha* and *Mahā-Vyūha Suttas*, Asoka says: "Concourse alone is best, that is, all should listen willingly to the doctrine professed by others."

Buddhism is not confined to any country or any particular nation. It is universal. It is not nationalism which, in other words, is another form of caste system founded on a wider basis. Buddhism, if it be permitted to say so, is super-nationalism.

To a Buddhist there is no far or near, no enemy or foreigner, no renegade or untouchable, since universal love realised through understanding has established the brotherhood of all living beings. A real Buddhist is a citizen of the world. He regards the whole world as his motherland and all as his brothers and sisters.

Buddhism is, therefore, unique, mainly owing to its tolerance, non-aggressiveness, rationality, practicability, efficacy and universality. It is the noblest of all unifying influences and the only lever that can uplift the world.

These are some of the salient features of Buddhism, and amongst some of the fundamental doctrines may be said—kamma or the law of moral causation, the doctrine of rebirth, anattā and Nibbāna.

Chapter 6

KAMMA OR THE LAW OF MORAL CAUSATION

We are faced with a totally ill-balanced world. We perceive the inequalities and manifold destinies of men and the numerous grades of beings that exist in the universe. We see one born into a condition of affluence, endowed with fine mental, moral and physical qualities and another into a condition of abject poverty and wretchedness. Here is a man virtuous and holy, but, contrary to his expectation, ill-luck is ever ready to greet him. The wicked world runs counter to his ambitions and desires. He is poor and miserable in spite of his honest dealings and piety. There is another vicious and foolish, but accounted to be fortune's darling. He is rewarded with all forms of favours, despite his shortcomings and evil modes of life.

Why, it may be questioned, should one be an inferior and another a superior? Why should one be wrested from the hands of a fond mother when one has scarcely seen a few summers, and another should perish in the flower of manhood, or at the ripe age of eighty or hundred? Why should one be sick and infirm, and another strong and healthy? Why should one be handsome, and another ugly and hideous, repulsive to all? Why should one be brought up in the lap of luxury, and another in absolute poverty, steeped in misery? Why should one be born a millionaire and another a pauper? Why should one be a mental prodigy, and another an idiot? Why should one be born with saintly characteristics, and another with criminal tendencies? Why should some be linguists, artists, mathematicians or musicians from the very cradle? Why should some be congenitally blind, deaf and deformed? Why should some be blessed and others cursed from their birth?

These are some problems that perplex the minds of all thinking men. How are we to account for all this unevenness of the world, this inequality of mankind?

Is it due to the work of blind chance or accident?

There is nothing in this world that happens by blind chance or accident. To say that anything happens by chance, is no more true than that this book has come here of itself. Strictly speaking, nothing happens to man that he does not deserve for some reason or other.

Could this be the fiat of an irresponsible Creator? Huxley writes:

"If we are to assume that anybody has designedly set this wonderful universe going, it is perfectly clear to me that he is no more entirely benevolent and just, in any intelligible sense of the words, than that he is malevolent and unjust."

According to Einstein:

"If this being (God) is omnipotent, then every occurrence, including every human action, every human thought, and every human feeling and aspiration is also his work; how is it possible to think of holding men responsible for their deeds and thoughts before such an Almighty Being?

"In giving out punishments and rewards, he would to a certain extent be passing judgment on himself. How can this be combined with the goodness and righteousness ascribed to him?

"According to the theological principles man is created arbitrarily and without his desire and at the moment of his creation is either blessed or damned eternally. Hence man is either good or evil, fortunate or unfortunate, noble or depraved, from the first step in the process of his physical creation to the moment of his last breath, regardless of his individual desires, hopes, ambitions, struggles or devoted prayers. Such is theological fatalism." (Spencer Lewis)

As Charles Bradlaugh says: "The existence of evil is a terrible stumbling block to the Theist. Pain, misery, crime,, poverty confront the advocate of eternal goodness and challenge with unanswerable potency his declaration of Deity as all-good, all-wise, and all-powerful."

In the words of Schopenhauer:

"Whoever regards himself as having become out of nothing must also think that he will again become nothing; for an eternity has passed before he was, and then a second eternity had begun, through which he will never cease to be, is a monstrous thought.

"If birth is the absolute beginning, then death must be his absolute end; and the assumption that man is made out of nothing leads necessarily to the assumption that death is his absolute end."

Commenting on human sufferings and God, Prof. J. B. S. Haldane writes:

"Either suffering is needed to perfect human character, or God is not Almighty. The former theory is disproved by the fact that some people who have suffered very little but have been fortunate in their ancestry and education have very fine characters. The objection to the second is that it is only in connection with the universe as a whole that there is any intellectual gap to be filled by the postulation of a deity. And a creator could presumably create whatever he or it wanted."

Lord Russell states:

"The world, we are told, was created by a God who is both good and omnipotent. Before he created the world he foresaw all the pain and misery that it would contain. He is therefore responsible for all of it. It is useless to argue that the pain in the world is due to sin.... If God knew in advance the sins of which man would be guilty, he was clearly responsible for all the consequences of those sins when he decided to create man."

In 'Despair,' a poem of his old age, Lord Tennyson thus boldly attacks God, who, as recorded in Isaiah, says,

"I make peace and create evil." (Isaiah, xiv. 7).

"What! I should call on that infinite love that has
served us so well?
Infinite cruelty, rather, that made everlasting
hell, Made us, foreknew us, foredoomed us, and
does what he will with his own.
Better our dead brute mother who never has
heard us groan."

Surely "the doctrine that all men are sinners and
have the essential sin of Adam is a challenge to
justice, mercy, love and omnipotent fairness."

Some writers of old authoritatively declared that
God created man in his own image. Some modern
thinkers state, on the contrary, that man created God
in his own image. With the growth of civilization
man's concept of God also became more and more
refined.

It is, however, impossible to conceive of such a
being either in or outside the universe.

Could this variation be due to heredity and
environment? One must admit that all such chemico-
physical phenomena revealed by scientists, are partly
instrumental, but they cannot be solely responsible
for the subtle distinctions and vast differences that
exist amongst individuals. Yet why should identical
twins who are physically alike, inheriting like genes,
enjoying the same privilege of upbringing, be very
often temperamentally, morally and intellectually
totally different?

Heredity alone cannot account for these vast
differences. Strictly speaking, it accounts more

plausibly for their similarities than for most of the differences. The infinitesimally minute chemico-physical germ, which is about 30 millionth part of an inch across, inherited from parents, explains only a portion of man, his physical foundation. With regard to the more, complex and subtle mental, intellectual and moral differences we need more enlightenment. The theory of heredity cannot give a satisfactory explanation for the birth of a criminal in a long line of honourable ancestors, the birth of a saint or a noble man in a family of evil repute, for the arising of infant prodigies, men of genius and great religious teachers.

According to Buddhism this variation is due not only to heredity, environment, "nature and nurture" but also to our own kamma, or in other words, to the result of our own inherited past actions and our present deeds. We ourselves are responsible for our own deeds, happiness and misery. We build our own hells. We create our own heavens. We are the architects of our own fate. In short we ourselves are our own kamma.[10]

On one occasion a certain young man named Subha approached the Buddha, and questioned why and wherefore it was that among human beings there are the low and high states.

"For," said he, "we find amongst mankind those of brief life and those of long life, the hale and the ailing, the good looking and the ill-looking, the

---

10. *Cūḷakammavibhaṅga Sutta—Majjhima Nikāya* No. 135.

powerful and the powerless, the poor and the rich, the low-born and the high-born, the ignorant and the intelligent."

The Buddha briefly replied: "Every living being has kamma as its own, its inheritance, its cause, its kinsman, its refuge. Kamma is that which differentiates all living beings into low and high states."

He then explained the cause of such differences in accordance with the law of moral causation.

Thus from a Buddhist standpoint, our present mental, intellectual, moral and temperamental differences are mainly due to our own actions and tendencies, both past and present.

Kamma, literally, means action; but, in its ultimate sense, it means the meritorious and demeritorious volition (*kusala akusala cetanā*). Kamma constitutes both good and evil. Good begets good. Evil begets evil. Like attracts like. This is the law of Kamma.

As some Westerners prefer to say, Kamma is "action influence."

We reap what we have sown. What we sow we reap somewhere or somewhen. In one sense we are the result of what we were; we will be the result of what we are. In another sense, we are not totally the result of what we were; we will not absolutely be the result of what we are. For instance, a criminal today may be a saint tomorrow.

Buddhism attributes this variation to Kamma, but it does not assert that everything is due to Kamma.

If everything were due to Kamma, a man must ever be bad for it is his Kamma to be bad. One need not consult a physician to be cured of a disease, for if one's Kamma is such one will be cured.

According to Buddhism, there are five orders or processes (*niyāmas*) which operate in the physical and mental realms:

i. *Kamma niyāma*, order of act and result, e.g., desirable and undesirable acts produce corresponding good and bad results.

ii. *Utu niyāma*, physical (inorganic) order; e.g., seasonal phenomena of winds and rains.

iii. *Bīja niyāma*, order of germs or seeds; (physical organic order), e.g., rice produced from rice-seed, sugary taste from sugar cane or honey etc. The scientific theory of cells and genes and the physical similarity of twins may be ascribed to this order.

iv. *Citta niyāma*, order of mind or psychic law, e.g., processes of consciousness (*cittavīthi*) power of mind, etc.

v. *Dhamma niyāma*, order of the norm, e.g. the natural phenomena occurring at the advent of a Bodhisatta in his last birth, gravitation, etc.

Every mental or physical phenomenon could be explained by these all-embracing five orders or processes which are laws in themselves.

Kamma is, therefore, only one of the five orders that prevail in the universe. It is a law in itself, but it does not thereby follow that there should be a law-giver. Ordinary laws of nature, like gravitation, need no law-giver. It operates in its own field without the intervention of an external,, independent ruling agency.

Nobody, for instance, has decreed that fire should burn. Nobody has commanded that water should seek its own level. No scientist has ordered that water should consist of H_2O, and that coldness should be one of its properties. These are their intrinsic characteristics. Kamma is neither fate nor predestination imposed upon us by some mysterious unknown power to which we must helplessly submit ourselves. It is one's own doing reacting on oneself, and so one has the possibility to divert the course of Kamma to some extent. How far one diverts it depends on oneself.

It must also be said that such phraseology as rewards and punishments should not be allowed to enter into discussions concerning the problem of Kamma. For Buddhism does not recognise an Almighty Being who rules his subjects and rewards and punishes them accordingly. Buddhists, on the contrary, believe that sorrow and happiness one experiences are the natural outcome of one's own good and bad actions. It should be stated that Kamma has both the continuative and the retributive principle.

Inherent in Kamma is the potentiality of producing its due effect. The cause produces the effect; the effect explains the cause. Seed produces the fruit; the fruit explains the seed as both are inter-related. Even so Kamma and its effect are inter-related; "the effect already blooms in the cause."

A Buddhist who is fully convinced of the doctrine of Kamma does not pray to another to be saved but confidently relies on himself for his purification because it teaches individual responsibility.

It is this doctrine of Kamma that gives him consolation, hope, self-reliance and moral courage. It is this belief in Kamma "that validates his effort, kindles his enthusiasm," makes him ever kind, tolerant and considerate. It is also this firm belief in Kamma that prompts him to refrain from evil, do good and be good without being frightened of any punishment or tempted by any reward.

It is this doctrine of Kamma that can explain the problem of suffering, the mystery of so-called fate or predestination of other religions, and above all the inequality of mankind. Kamma and rebirth are accepted as axiomatic.

Chapter 7

REBIRTH

As long as this Kammic force exists there is rebirth, for beings are merely the visible manifestation of this invisible Kammic force. Death is nothing but the temporary end of this temporary phenomenon. It is not the complete annihilation of this so-called being. The organic life has ceased, but the Kammic force which hitherto actuated it has not been destroyed. As the Kammic force remains entirely undisturbed by the disintegration of the fleeting body, the passing away of the present dying thought-moment only conditions a fresh consciousness in another birth.

It is Kamma, rooted in ignorance and craving, that conditions rebirth. Past Kamma conditions the present birth; and present Kamma, in combination with past Kamma, conditions the future. The present is the offspring of the past, and becomes, in turn, the parent of the future.

If we postulate a past, present, and a future life, then we are at once faced with the alleged mysterious problem 'What is the ultimate origin of life?'

Either there must be a beginning or there cannot be a beginning for life.

One school, in attempting to solve the problem, postulates a first cause, God, viewed as a force or as an Almighty Being. Another school denies a first cause for, in common experience, the cause ever becomes the effect and the effect becomes the cause. In a circle of cause and effect a first cause is inconceivable. According to the former, life has had a beginning; according to the latter, it is beginningless.

From the scientific standpoint, we are the direct products of the sperm and ovum cells provided by our parents. As such life precedes life. With regard to the origin of the first protoplasm of life, or colloid, scientists plead ignorance.

According to Buddhism we are born from the matrix of action (*kammayoni*). Parents merely provide an infinitesimally small cell. As such being precedes being. At the moment of conception it is past Kamma that conditions the initial consciousness that vitalizes the foetus. It is this invisible Kammic energy, generated from the past birth that produces mental phenomena and the phenomenon of life in an already extant physical phenomenon, to complete the trio that constitutes man.

For a being to be born here a being must die somewhere. The birth of a being, which strictly means the arising of the five aggregates or psycho-physical phenomena in this present life, corresponds to the death of a being in a past life; just as, in conventional terms, the rising of the sun in one place means the setting of the sun in another place. This enigmatic statement may be better understood by imagining life as a wave and not as a straight line. Birth and death are only two phases of the same process. Birth precedes death, and death, on the other hand, precedes birth. This constant succession of birth and death in connection with each individual life flux constitutes what is technically known as *saṃsāra*—recurrent wandering.

What is the ultimate origin of life?

The Buddha declares:

"Without cognizable end is this *saṃsāra*. A first beginning of beings, who, obstructed by ignorance and fettered by craving, wander and fare on, is not to be perceived."

This life-stream flows *ad infinitum*, as long as it is fed by the muddy waters of ignorance and craving. When these two are completely cut off, then only, if one so wishes, does the stream cease to flow; rebirth ends as in the case of the Buddhas and Arahants. An ultimate beginning of this life-stream cannot be determined, as a stage cannot be perceived when this life-force was not fraught with ignorance and craving.

The Buddha has here referred merely to the beginning of the life-stream of living beings. It is left to scientists to speculate on the origin and the evolution of the universe. The Buddha does not attempt to solve all the ethical and philosophical problems that perplex mankind. Nor does he deal with theories and speculations that tend neither to edification nor to enlightenment. Nor does he demand blind faith from his adherents. He is chiefly concerned with the problem of suffering and its destruction. With but this one practical and specific purpose in view, all irrelevant side issues are completely ignored.

But how are we to believe that there is a past existence?

The most valuable evidence Buddhists cite in favour of rebirth is the Buddha, for he developed a knowledge which enabled him to read past and future lives.

Following his instructions, his disciples also developed this knowledge and were able to read their past lives to a great extent.

Even some Indian Rishis, before the advent of the Buddha, were distinguished for such psychic powers as clairaudience, clairvoyance, thought-reading, remembering past births, etc.

There are also some persons, who, probably in accordance with the laws of association, spontaneously develop the memory of their past birth, and remember fragments of their previous lives. Such cases are very rare, but those few well-attested,, respectable cases tend to throw some light on the idea of a past birth. So are the experiences of some modern dependable psychics and strange cases of alternating and multiple personalities.

In hypnotic states some relate experiences of their past lives; while a few others, read the past lives of others and even heal diseases.[11]

Sometimes we get strange experiences which cannot be explained but by rebirth.

How often do we meet persons whom we have never met,, and yet instinctively feel that they are quite familiar to us? How often do we visit places, and yet feel impressed that we are perfectly acquainted with those surroundings?

The Buddha tells us:

"Through previous associations or present advantage, that old love springs up again like the lotus in the water." Experiences of some reliable modern psychists, ghostly phenomena, spirit communications, strange alternating and multiple personalities and so on shed some light upon this problem of rebirth.

Into this world come perfect Ones like the Buddhas and highly developed personalities. Do they evolve suddenly? Can they be the products of a single existence?

How are we to account for great characters like Buddhaghosa, Pāṇini, Kālidāsa, Homer and Plato, men of genius like Shakespeare, infant prodigies like Pascal, Mozart, Beethoven, Raphael, Rāmanujan, etc?

Heredity alone cannot account for them. "Else their ancestry would disclose it, their posterity, even greater than themselves, demonstrate it."

Could they rise to such lofty heights if they had not lived. noble lives and gained similar experiences in the past? Is it by mere chance that they are been

---

11. See—*Many Mansions and The World Within* by Gina Cerminara

born of those particular parents and placed under those favourable circumstances?

The few years that we are privileged to spend here, or for the most five score years, must certainly be an inadequate preparation for eternity.

If one believes in the present and in the future, it is quite logical to believe in the past. The present is the offspring of the past, and acts in turn as the parent of the future.

If there are reasons to believe that we have existed in the past, then surely there are no reasons to disbelieve that we shall. continue to exist after our present life has apparently ceased.

It is indeed a strong argument in favour of past and future lives that "in this world virtuous persons are very often, unfortunate and vicious persons prosperous."

A Western writer says:

"Whether we believe in a past existence or not, it forms the only reasonable hypothesis which bridges certain gaps in, human knowledge concerning certain facts of every day life. Our reason tells us that this idea of past birth and Kamma alone can explain the degrees of difference that exist between, twins, how men like Shakespeare with a very limited experience are able to portray with marvelous exactitude the most diverse types of human character, scenes and so forth of which they could have no actual knowledge, why the work of the genius invariably transcends his experience, the existence of infant precocity, the vast diversity in mind and morals, in brain and physique, in conditions, circumstances and environment observable throughout the world, and so forth."

It should be stated that this doctrine of rebirth can neither 'be proved nor disproved experimentally, but it is accepted as an evidentially verifiable fact.

The cause of this Kamma, continues the Buddha, is *avijjā* or ignorance of the Four Noble Truths. Ignorance is, therefore, the cause of birth and death; and its transmutation into knowingness or *vijjā* is consequently their cessation.

The result of this analytical method is summed up in dependent origination, *paṭicca samuppāda*.

Chapter 8

DEPENDENT ORIGINATION, *Paṭicca samuppāda*

Paṭicca means because of, or dependent upon. *Samuppāda* "arising or origination." *Paṭicca samuppada*, therefore, literally means "dependent arising" or "dependent origination."

It must be borne in mind that *paṭicca samuppāda*, is only a discourse on the process of birth and death and not a theory of the ultimate origin of life. It deals with the cause of rebirth and suffering, but it does not in the least attempt to show the evolution of the world from primordial matter.

Ignorance (*avijjā*) is the first link or cause of the wheel of life. It clouds all right understanding.

Dependent on ignorance of the Four Noble Truths arise activities (*saṅkhārā*)—both moral and immoral. The activities, whether good or bad rooted in ignorance which must necessarily have their due effects only tend to prolong life's wandering. Nevertheless, good actions are essential to get rid of the ills of life.

Dependent on activities arises rebirth consciousness. (*viññāṇa*). This links the past with the present. Simultaneous. with the arising of rebirth-consciousness there come into being mind and body (*nāma-rūpa*).

The six senses (*saḷāyatana*) are the inevitable consequences, of mind and body.

Because of the six senses contact (*phassa*) sets in. Contact leads to feeling (*vedanā*).

These five, viz., consciousness, mind and matter, six senses, contact and feeling are the effects of past actions and are called the passive side of life.

Dependent on feeling arises craving (*taṇhā*). Craving results in grasping (*upādāna*). Grasping is the cause of kamma (*bhava*) which in its turn, conditions future birth (*jāti*). Birth is the inevitable cause of old age and death (*jarā-maraṇa*).

If on account of cause effect comes to be, then if the cause ceases, the effect also must cease.

The reverse order of the *paṭicca samuppāda* will make the matter clear.

Old age and death are possible in, and with, a psychophysical organism. Such an organism must be born; therefore it pre-supposes birth. But birth is the inevitable result of past deeds or Kamma. Kamma is conditioned by grasping which is due to craving. Such craving can appear only where feeling exists. Feeling is the outcome of contact between the senses and objects. Therefore it presupposes organs of senses which cannot exist without mind and body. Where there is a mind there is consciousness. It is the result of past good and evil. The acquisition of good and ,evil is due to ignorance of things as they truly are. The whole formula may be summed up thus:

Dependent on ignorance arise activities (moral and immoral)

" " Activities arises consciousness (rebirth consciousness)

" " Consciousness arise mind and matter.

" " Mind and matter arise the six spheres of sense.

" " the six spheres of sense arises contact.

" " Contact arises feeling. '

" " Feeling arises craving.

" " Craving arises grasping

" " Grasping arise actions (kamma)

" " Actions arises rebirth

" " Birth arise decay, death, sorrow, lamentation, pain, grief and despair.

Thus does the entire aggregate of suffering arise. The first two of these twelve pertain to the past, the middle eight to the present, and the last two to the future.

The complete cessation of ignorance leads to the cessation of activities.

The cessation of activities leads to, the cessation of consciousness.

" " Consciousness leads to the cessation of mind and matter.

" " Mind and matter leads to the cessation of the six spheres of sense.

" " the six spheres of sense leads to the cessation of contact.

" " Contact leads to the cessation of feeling.
" " Feeling leads to the cessation of craving.
" " Craving leads to the cessation of grasping.
" " Grasping leads to the cessation of actions.
" " Actions leads to the cessation of rebirth.
" " Rebirth leads to the cessation of decay, death, sorrow, lamentation, pain, grief, and despair.

Thus does the cessation of this entire aggregate of suffering result.

This process of cause and effect continues ad infinitum. The beginning of this process cannot be determined as it is impossible to say whence this life-flux was encompassed by nescience. But when this nescience is turned into knowledge, and the life-flux is diverted into the *Nibbānadhātu*, then the end of the life process or *saṃsāra* comes about.

Chapter 9

ANATTĀ OR SOULLESSNESS

This Buddhist doctrine of rebirth should be distinguished from the theory of re-incarnation which implies the transmigration of a soul and its invariable material rebirth. Buddhism denies the existence of an unchanging or eternal soul created by a God or emanating from a Divine Essence (*Paramātma*).

If the immortal soul, which is supposed to be the essence of man, is eternal, there cannot be either a rise or a fall. Besides one cannot understand why "different souls are so variously constituted at the outset."

To prove the existence of endless felicity in an eternal. heaven and unending torments in an eternal hell, an immortal soul is absolutely necessary. Otherwise, what is it that is punished in hell or rewarded in heaven?

"It should be said," writes Bertrand Russell, "that the old distinction between soul and body has evaporated quite as much because "matter" has lost its solidity as mind has lost its spirituality. Psychology is just beginning to be scientific. In the present state of psychology belief in immortality can at any rate claim no support from science."

Buddhists do agree with Russell when he says "there is obviously some reason in which I am the same person as I was yesterday, and, to take an even more obvious example, if I simultaneously see a man and hear him speaking, there is some sense in which the 'I' that sees is the same as the that hears."

Till recently scientists believed in an indivisible and indestructible atom. "For sufficient reasons physicists have reduced this atom to a series of events. For equally good reasons psychologists find that mind has not the identity of a single continuing thing but is a series of occurrences bound together by certain intimate relations. The question of immortality, therefore, has become the question whether these intimate relations exist between occurrences connected with a living body and other occurrences which take place after that body is dead."

As C. E. M. Joad says in *The Meaning of Life*, matter has since disintegrated under our very eyes. It is no longer solid; it is no longer enduring; it is no longer determined by compulsive causal laws; and more important than all, it is no longer known. The so-called atoms, it seems, are both 'divisible and destructible.' The electrons and protons that compose atoms 'can meet and annihilate one another while their persistence, such as it is, is rather that of a wave lacking fixed boundaries, and in process of continual change both as regards shape and position than that of a thing.'

Bishop Berkeley who showed that this so-called atom is a metaphysical fiction held that there exists a spiritual substance called the soul.

Hume, for instance, looked into consciousness and perceived that there was nothing except fleeting mental states and concluded that the supposed 'permanent ego' is nonexistent.

"There are some philosophers," he says, "who imagine we are every moment conscious of what we call 'ourself' that we feel its existence and its continuance in existence and so we are certain … both of its perfect identity and simplicity. For my part, when I enter most intimately into what I call 'myself' I always stumble on some particular perception or other—of heat or cold, light or shade, love or hatred, pain or pleasure. I never catch myself … and never can observe anything but the perception … nor do I conceive what is further requisite to make me a perfect non-entity."

Bergson says, "All consciousness is time existence; and a conscious state is not a state that endures without changing. It is a change without ceasing; when change ceases it ceases; it is itself nothing but change."

Dealing with this question of soul Prof. James says—"The soul-theory is a complete superfluity, so far as accounting for the actually verified facts of conscious experience goes. So far no one can be compelled to subscribe to it for definite scientific reasons." In concluding his interesting chapter on the soul he says: "And in this book the provisional solution which we have reached must be the final word: the thoughts themselves are the thinkers."

Watson, a distinguished psychologist, states: "No one has ever touched a soul or has seen one in a test tube, or has in any way come into relationship with it as he has with the other objects of his daily experience. Nevertheless to doubt its existence is to become a heretic and once might possibly even had led to the loss of one's head. Even today a man holding a public position dare not question it."

The Buddha anticipated these facts some 2500 years ago. According to Buddhism mind is nothing but a complex compound of fleeting mental states. One unit of consciousness consists of three phases— arising or genesis (*uppāda*) static or development (*ṭhīṭṭhiti*), and cessation or dissolution (*bhaṅga*). Immediately after the cessation stage of a thought moment there occurs the genesis stage of the subsequent thought-moment. Each momentary consciousness of this ever-changing life-process, on passing away, transmits its whole energy, all the indelibly recorded impressions to its successor. Every fresh consciousness consists of the potentialities of its predecessors together with something more. There is, therefore, a continuous flow of consciousness like a stream without any interruption. The subsequent thought-moment is neither absolutely the same as its predecessor since that which goes to make it up is not identical—nor entirely another—being the same continuity of Kamma energy. Here there is no identical being but there is an identity in process.

Every moment there is birth, every moment there is death. The arising of one thought-moment means the passing away of another thought-moment and vice versa. In the course of one life-time there is momentary rebirth without a soul.

It must not be understood that a consciousness is chopped up in bits and joined together like a train or a chain. But, on the contrary, "it persistently flows on like a river receiving from the tributary streams of sense constant accretions to its flood, and ever dispensing to the world without it the thought stuff it has gathered by the way."[12] It has birth for its source and death for its mouth. The rapidity of the flow is such that hardly is there any standard whereby it can be measured even approximately. However, it pleases the commentators to say that the time duration of one thought-moment is even less than one-billionth part of the time occupied by a flash of lightning.

Here we find a juxtaposition of such fleeting mental states of consciousness opposed to a super-position of such states as some appear to believe. No state once gone ever recurs nor is identical with what goes before. But we worldlings, veiled by the web of illusion, mistake this apparent continuity to be something eternal and go to the extent of introducing an unchanging soul, an Atta, the supposed doer and

---

12. See *Compendium of Philosophy,* Introduction p. 12

receptacle of all actions to this ever-changing consciousness.

"The so-called being is like a flash of lightning that is resolved into a succession of sparks that follow upon one another with such rapidity that the human retina cannot perceive them separately, nor can the uninstructed conceive of such succession of separate sparks"[13] As the wheel of a cart rests on the ground at one point, so does the being live only for one thought-moment. It is always in the present, and is ever slipping into the irrevocable past. What we shall become is determined by this present thought-moment.

If there is no soul, what is it that is reborn? one might ask. Well, there is nothing to be re-born. When life ceases the Kammic energy rematerialises itself in another form. As Bhikkhu Sīlācāra says: "Unseen it passes whithersoever the conditions appropriate to its visible manifestation are present. Here showing itself as a tiny gnat or worm, there making its presence known in the dazzling magnificence of a Deva or an Archangel's existence. When one mode of its manifestation ceases it merely passes on, and where suitable circumstances offer, reveals itself afresh in another name or form."

---

13. Compare the cinematograph film where individual photographs give rise to a notion of movement.

Birth is the arising of the psycho-physical phenomena. Death is merely the temporary end of a temporary phenomenon.

Just as the arising of a physical state is conditioned by a preceding state as its cause, so the appearance of psychophysical phenomena is conditioned by causes anterior to its birth. As the process of one life-span is possible without a permanent entity passing from one thought-moment to another, so a series of life-processes is possible without an immortal soul to transmigrate from one existence to another.

Buddhism does not totally deny the existence of a personality in an empirical sense. It only attempts to show that it does not exist in an ultimate sense. The Buddhist philosophical term for an individual is *santāna*, i.e., a flux or a continuity. It includes the mental and physical elements as well. The kammic force of each individual binds the elements together. This uninterrupted flux or continuity of psychophysical phenomenon, which is conditioned by kamma—and not limited only to the present life, but having its source in the beginningless past and its continuation in the future—is the Buddhist substitute for the permanent ego or the immortal soul of other religions.

Chapter 10

NIBBĀNA

This process of birth and death continues *ad infinitum* until this flux is transmuted, so to say, to Nibbānadhātu, the ultimate goal of Buddhists.

The Pali word *Nibbāna* is formed of *nir* and *vāna*. *Nir* is a negative particle and *vāna* means lusting or craving. "It is called *Nibbāna*, in that it is a departure from the craving which is called *Vāna* lusting." Literally, *Nibbāna* means non-attachment.

It may also be defined as the extinction of lust, hatred and ignorance. "The whole world is in flames," says the Buddha. "By what fire is it kindled? By the fire of lust, hatred and ignorance, by the fire of birth, old age, death, pain, lamentation, sorrow, grief and despair it is kindled."

It should not be understood that Nibbāna, is a state of nothingness or annihilation owing to the fact that we cannot perceive it with our worldly knowledge. One cannot say that there exists no light just because the blind man does not see it. In that well known story, too, the fish arguing with his friend, the turtle, triumphantly concluded that there exists no land.

Nibbāna of the Buddhists is neither a mere nothingness nor a state of annihilation, but what it is no words can adequately express. Nibbāna is a Dhamma which is "unborn, unoriginated, uncreated, and unformed." Hence it is eternal (*dhuva*), desirable (*subha*), and happy (*sukha*).

In Nibbāna nothing is "eternalised," nor is anything "annihilated," besides suffering.

According to the Books references are made to Nibbāna as *sopādisesa* and *anupādisesa*. These, in fact, are not two kinds of Nibbāna, but the one single Nibbāna, receiving its name according to the way it is experienced before and after death.

Nibbāna is not situated in any place nor is it a sort of heaven where a transcendental ego resides. It is a state which is dependent upon this body itself. It is an attainment (Dhamma) which is within the reach of all. Nibbāna is a supramundane state attainable even in this present life. Buddhism does not state that this ultimate goal could be reached only in a life beyond. Here lies the chief difference between the Buddhist conception of Nibbāna and the non-Buddhist conception of an eternal heaven attainable only after death or a union with a God or Divine Essence in an after-life. When Nibbāna is realized in this life with the body remaining, it is called *Sopādisesa Nibbāna-dhātu*. When an Arahant attains Parinibbāna, after the dissolution of his body, without any remainder of physical existence it is called *Anupādisesa Nibbāna-dhātu*. In the words of Sir Edwin Arnold—

> "If any teach Nirvana is to cease
> Say unto such they lie.
> If any teach Nirvana is to live
> Say unto such they err."

From a metaphysical standpoint Nibbāna is deliverance from suffering. From a psychological standpoint Nibbāna is the eradication of egoism. From an ethical standpoint Nibbāna is the destruction of lust, hatred and ignorance.

Does the Arahant exist or not after death?

The Buddha replies—"The Arahant who has been released from the five aggregates is deep, immeasurable like the mighty ocean. To say that he is reborn would not fit the case. To say that he is neither reborn nor not reborn would not &t the case."

One cannot say that an Arahant is reborn as all passions that condition rebirth are eradicated ; nor can one say that the Arahant is annihilated for there is nothing to annihilate. Robert Oppenheimer, a scientist, writes:

"If we ask, for instance, whether the position of the electron remains the same, we must say 'no'; if we ask whether the electron's position changes with time, we must say 'no'; if we ask whether the electron is at rest, we must say 'no'; if we ask whether it is in motion, we must say 'no.'

"The Buddha has given such answers when interrogated as to the conditions of man's self after death;[14] but they are not familiar answers from the tradition of 'the 17th and 18th century science."

---

14. Evidently the writer is referring to the state of an Arahat after death.

Chapter 11

THE PATH TO NIBBĀNA

How is Nibbāna to be attained?

It is by following the Noble Eight-fold Path which consists of Right Understanding (*Sammā-Diṭṭhi*), Right Thoughts (*Sammā-Saṅkappa*), Right Speech (*Sammā-Vācā*), Right Actions (*Sammā-Kammanta*), Right Livelihood (*Sammā-Ājīva*), Right Effort (*Sammā-Vāyāma*), Right Mindfulness (*Sammā-Sati*) and Right Concentration (*Sammā-Samādhi*).

This unique Path constitutes Morality (*Sīla*), Concentration (*Samādhi*), and Wisdom (*Paññā*).

The Buddha summarises his Middle Way in the following beautiful little verse:

> *Sabba pāpassa akaraṇaṃ*
> *Kusalassa upasampadā*
> *Sacitta-pariyodapanaṃ*
> *Etaṃ Buddhāna sāsanaṃ*

> To refrain from all evil,
> To do what is good,
> To cleanse one's mind,
> This is the advice of all Buddhas.

Morality (*sīla*) is the first stage on this path to Nibbāna. Without killing or causing injury to any living creature, he should be kind and compassionate towards all, even to the tiniest creature that crawls at

68

his feet. Refraining from stealing, he should be upright and honest in all his dealings. Abstaining from sexual misconduct which debases the exalted nature of man, he should be pure. Shunning false speech,, he should be truthful. Avoiding pernicious drinks that promote heedlessness, he should be sober and diligent.

These elementary principles of regulated behaviour are essential to one who treads the path to Nibbāna. Violation of them means the introduction of obstacles on the path which will obstruct his moral progress. Observance of them means steady and smooth progress along the path.

The spiritual pilgrim, disciplining thus his words and deeds, may advance a step further and try to control. his senses.

While he progresses slowly and steadily with regulated word and deed and restrained senses, the Kammic force of this striving aspirant may compel him to renounce worldly pleasures and adopt the ascetic life. To him then comes the idea that

"A den of strife is household life,
And filled with toil and need;
But free and high as the open sky.
Is the life the homeless lead."

It should not be understood that everyone is expected to lead the life of a Bhikkhu or a celibate life to achieve one's goal. One's spiritual progress is expedited by being a Bhikkhu although as a lay follower one can become an Arahant. After attaining the third stage of Sainthood, one leads a life of celibacy.

Securing a firm footing on the ground of morality, the progressing pilgrim then embarks upon the higher practice of *samādhi*, the control and culture of the mind—the second stage on this Path.

Samādhi—is the "one-pointedness of the mind." It is the concentration of the mind on one object to the entire exclusion of all irrelevant matter.

There are different subjects for meditation according to the temperaments of the individuals. Concentration on respiration is the easiest to gain the one-pointedness of the mind. Meditation on loving-kindness is very beneficial as it is conducive to mental peace and happiness.

Cultivation of the four sublime states—loving-kindness (*mettā*), compassion (*karuṇā*), sympathetic joy (*muditā*), and equanimity (*upekkhā*) is highly commendable.

After giving careful consideration to the subject for contemplation, he should choose the one most suited to his temperament. This being satisfactorily settled, he makes a persistent effort to focus his mind until he becomes so wholly absorbed and interested in it, that all other thoughts get ipso facto excluded from the mind. The five hindrances to progress— namely, sense-desire, hatred, sloth and torpor, restlessness and brooding and doubts are then temporarily inhibited. Eventually he gains ecstatic concentration and, to his indescribable joy, becomes enwrapt in jhāna, enjoying the calmness .and serenity of a one-pointed-mind.

When one gains this perfect one-pointedness of the mind it is possible for one to develop the five It supernormal powers (*abhiññā*)—divine eye, (*dibbacakkhu*), divine ear (*dibbasota*), reminiscence of past births (*pubbenivāsānussati ñāna*), thought reading (*paracitta vijānana*), and different psychic powers (*iddhividha*). must not be understood that those supernormal powers are essential for Sainthood. Though the mind is now purified there still lies dormant in him the tendency to give vent to his passions, for, by concentration, passions are lulled to sleep temporarily. They may rise to the surface at unexpected moments.

Both discipline and concentration are helpful to clear the Path of its obstacles but it is Insight (*vipassanā paññā*) alone which enables one to see things as they truly are, and consequently reach the ultimate goal by completely annihilating the passions inhibited by concentration. This is the third and the final stage on the Path to Nibbāna.

With his one-pointed mind which now resembles a polished mirror he looks at the world to get a correct view of life, Wherever he turns his eyes he sees nought but the three characteristics—*anicca* (transiency), *dukkha* (sorrow) and *anattā* (soullessness) standing out in bold relief. He comprehends that life is constantly changing and all conditioned things are transient. Neither in heaven nor on earth does he find any genuine happiness, for every form of pleasure is a prelude to, pain. What is transient is therefore painful, and where change and sorrow prevail, there cannot be a permanent immortal soul.

Whereupon, of these three characteristics, he chooses one that appeals to him most and intently keeps on developing Insight in that particular direction until that glorious day comes to him when he would realize Nibbāna for the first time in his life, having destroyed the three fetters—self-illusion (*sakkāya-diṭṭhi*), doubts (*vicikicchā*), indulgence in (wrongful) rites and ceremonies (*sīlabbataparāmāsa*).

At this stage he is called a *Sotāpanna* (Stream-Winner)—one who has entered the stream that leads to Nibbāna. As. he has not eradicated all fetters he is reborn seven times at the most.

Summoning up fresh courage, as a result of this glimpse of Nibbāna, the Aryan Pilgrim makes rapid progress and cultivating deeper Insight becomes a *Sakadāgāmi*—(Once Returner)—by weakening two more Fetters—namely, Sense-desire (*kāmarāga*) and ill-will (*paṭigha*). He is called a Sakadāgāmi because he is reborn on earth only once in case he does not attain Arahantship.

It is in the third stage of Sainthood—*Anāgāmi* (Never-Returner) that he completely discards the aforesaid two Fetters. Thereafter, he neither returns to this world nor does he seek birth in the celestial realms, since he has no more desire for sensual pleasures. After death he is reborn in the "Pure Abodes" (*suddhāvāsa*), a congenial Brahma plane, till he attains Arahantship.

Now the saintly pilgrim, encouraged by the unprecedented success of his endeavours, makes his final advance and destroying the remaining fetters, namely, lust after life in realms of forms (*rūparāga*) and formless realms (*arūparāga*), ,conceit (*māna*), restlessness (*uddhacca*), and ignorance (*avijjā*) becomes a perfect Saint—an Arahant, a Worthy One.

Instantly he realizes that what was to be accomplished has been done, that a heavy burden of sorrow has been relinquished, that all forms of attachment have been totally annihilated, and that the Path to Nibbāna has been trodden. The Worthy-One now stands on heights more than celestial, far removed from the rebellious passions and defilements of the world, realizing the unutterable bliss of Nibbāna and like many an Arahant of old, uttering that paeon of joy:

> "Goodwill and wisdom, mind by method trained,
> The highest conduct on good morals based,
> This makes mortals pure, not rank or wealth."

As T. H. Huxley states—"Buddhism is a system which knows no God in the Western sense, which denies a soul to man, which counts the belief in immortality a blunder, which refuses any efficacy to prayer and sacrifice, which bids men to look to nothing but their own efforts for salvation, which in its original purity knew nothing of vows of obedience and never sought the aid of the secular arm: yet spread over a considerable moiety of the world with marvellous rapidity—and is still the dominant creed of a large fraction of mankind."

APPENDIX

Concentration on Respiration
Ānāpāna-sati

Ānāpāna-sati is mindfulness on respiration. *Āna* means inhalation and *apāna*, exhalation.

Concentration on the breathing process leads to one pointedness of the mind and ultimately to Insight which enables one to attain Sainthood or Arahantship.

The Buddha also practised concentration on respiration before he attained Enlightenment.

This harmless concentration may be practised by any person, irrespective of religious beliefs.

Adopting a convenient posture, keep the body erect. Place the right hand over the left hand. Eyes may be closed or half-closed.

Easterners generally sit cross-legged with the body erect. They sit placing the right foot on the left thigh and the left foot on the right thigh. This is the full position. Sometimes they adopt the half position, that is by simply placing the right foot on the left thigh or the left foot on the right thigh.

When the triangular position is assumed the whole body is well-balanced.

Those who find the cross-legged posture too difficult may sit comfortably in a chair or any other support sufficiently high to rest the legs on the ground.

It is of no importance which posture one may adopt provided the position is easy and relaxed.

Head should not be drooping. Neck should be straightened so that the nose may be in a perpendicular line with the navel.

Buddhas usually adopt the full lotus position. They sit with half closed eyes looking not more than a distance of three and half feet.

Before the practice, bad air from the lungs should be breathed out slowly through the mouth and then the mouth should be closed.

Now inhale through the nostrils normally, without strain, without force. Mentally count one. Exhale and count two. Inhale and count three. Count up to ten constantly concentrating on the breathing process without thinking of anything else. While doing so one's mind may wander. But, ,one need not be discouraged. Gradually one may increase the number of series-say five series of ten.

Later, one may inhale and pause for a moment, concentrating merely on inhalation without counting. Exhale and pause for a moment. Thus inhale and exhale concentrating on respiration. Some prefer counting as it aids concentration while others prefer not to count. What is essential is concentration and not counting which is secondary.

When one practises this concentration one feels very peaceful, light in mind and body. After practising for a certain period a day might come when one may realize that this so-called body is supported by mere breath and that body perishes when breathing ceases. One fully realizes impermanence. Where there is change there cannot be a permanent entity or an immortal soul. Insight can then be developed to attain Arahantship.

It is clear that the object of this concentration on respiration is not merely to gain one-pointedness but also to cultivate + Insight to obtain deliverance from suffering.

In some discourses this simple and harmless method of respiration is described as follows:

"Mindfully he inhales; mindfully he exhales."

1. When making a long inhalation he knows: 'I make a long inhalation'; when making a long exhalation he knows: 'I make a long exhalation.'

2. When making a short inhalation he knows: 'I make a short inhalation' when making a short exhalation he knows: 'I make a short exhalation.'

3. Clearly perceiving the entire breathing process (i.e., the beginning, middle and end), 'I will inhale': thus he trains himself; clearly perceiving the entire breathing process, 'I will exhale': thus he trains himself.

4. Calming the respirations, 'I will inhale: thus he trains himself; calming the respirations, 'I will exhale': thus he trains himself.

MEDITATION ON LOVING-KINDNESS (*Mettā*)

Be still and peaceful.

Recite three times—*Namo Buddhāya*—(Honour to the Buddha) Recite three times—*Arahaṃ*—(The Pure One)

Recite

Buddhaṃ saraṇaṃ gacchāmi—
(I go to the Buddha for refuge)
Dhammaṃ saraṇaṃ gacchāmi—
(I go to the Dhamma for refuge)
Saṅghaṃ saraṇaṃ gacchāmi—
(I go to the Sangha for refuge)[15]

*   *   *

Think thus

My mind is temporarily pure, free from all impurities; free from lust, hatred and ignorance; free from all evil thoughts.

My mind is pure and clean. Like a polished mirror is my stainless mind.

As a clean and empty vessel is filled with pure water I now fill my clean heart and pure mind with peaceful and sublime thoughts of boundless loving-

---

15. This introductory part may be deleted by non-Buddhists.

kindness, overflowing compassion, sympathetic joy and perfect equanimity.

I have now washed my mind and heart of anger, ill-will, cruelty, violence, jealousy, envy, passion and aversion.

Think ten times—

May I[16] be well and happy!

May I be free from suffering, disease, grief, worry and anger! May I be strong, self-confident, healthy and peaceful! Think thus—

Now I charge every particle of my system, from head to foot, with thoughts of boundless loving-kindness and compassion. I am the embodiment of loving-kindness and compassion. My whole body is saturated with loving-kindness and compassion. I am a stronghold, a fortress. of loving-kindness and compassion. I am nothing but loving-kindness and compassion. I 'have sublimated . myself, elevated myself, ennobled myself.

Think ten times—

May I be well and happy!

May I be free from suffering, disease, grief, worry and. anger!

May I be strong, self-confident, healthy and peaceful! Think:

Mentally I create an aura of loving-kindness around me. By means of this aura, I cut off all negative thoughts, hostile vibrations. I am not

---

16.   Here the term "I" is used in a conventional sense.

affected by the evil vibrations of others. I return good for evil, loving-kindness for anger, compassion for cruelty, sympathetic joy for jealousy. I am peaceful and well-balanced in mind.

Now I am a fortress of loving-kindness, a stronghold of morality.

What I have gained I now give unto others.

Think of all your near and dear ones at home, individually or collectively, and fill them with thoughts of loving-kindness, and wish them peace and happiness, repeating May all beings be well and happy! ... Then think of all seen and unseen beings, living near and far, men, women, animals and all living beings, in the East, West, North, South, above and below, and radiate boundless loving-kindness, without any enmity or obstruction, towards all, irrespective of class, creed, colour or sex.

Think that all are your brothers and sisters, fellow-beings in the ocean of life. You identify yourself with all. You are one with all.

Repeat ten times—"May all beings be well and happy..." and wish them all peace and happiness.

In the course of your daily life try to translate your thoughts into action as occasion demands.

PERFECTIONS (*Pāramī*)

1. May I be generous and helpful! (*dāna-pāramī*—perfection of generosity)

2. May I be well-disciplined and refined in manners! May I be pure and clean in all my dealings! May my thoughts, words and deeds be pure! (*sīla-pāramī*—perfection of morality)

3. May I not be selfish and self-possessive but selfless and disinterested! May I be able to sacrifice my pleasures for the sake of others! (*nekkhamma*—renunciation)

4. May I be wise and be able to see things as they truly are! May I see the light of Truth and lead others from darkness to light! May I be enlightened and be able to enlighten others! May I be able to give the benefit of my knowledge to others! (*paññā*—wisdom)

5. May I be energetic, vigorous and persevering! May I strive diligently until I achieve my goal! May I be fearless in facing dangers and courageously surmount all obstacles! May I be able to serve others to the best of my ability! (*viriya*—energy)

6. May I ever be patient! May I be able to bear and forbear the wrongs of others! May I ever be tolerant and see the good and beautiful in all! (*khanti*—patience)

7. May I ever be truthful and honest! May I not hide the truth to be polite! May I never swerve from the path of Truth! (*sacca*—truthfulness).

8. May I be firm and resolute and have an iron will! May I be soft as a flower and firm as a rock! May I ever be high-principled! (*adhiṭṭṭhāna*—determination).

9. May I ever be kind, friendly and compassionate! May I be able to regard all as my brothers and sisters and be one with all! (*mettā*—loving-kindness)

10. May I ever be calm, serene, unruffled and peaceful! May—I gain a balanced mind! May I have perfect equanimity! (*upekkhā*—equanimity).

May I serve to be perfect! May I be perfect to serve!

MEDITATION ON "I"

Contemplate—Who am "I"?

Is there an "I"?

The so-called "I" is the source of all troubles, worries, unrest and unhappiness.

When "I" clings to a desirable object there arises attachment or affection.

When "I" is averse to an undesirable object there arise ill-will, anger or hatred.

When "I" is frustrated there arise pain, grief, worry, remorse, unhappiness which might ultimately end in suicide or murder.

When "I" is in danger there arises fear.

When "I" is confined to oneself there arise selfishness, separatism, jealousy, envy.

When "I" is puffed up there arises pride or conceit. When "I" is expanded and is merged in the whole there arise selflessness,, non-separatism, boundless compassion, universal loving-kindness and perfect harmony, When "I" is crossed or transcended there arise perfect equilibrium and equanimity with no attachment or aversion.

QUOTATIONS

"Happiness is non-attachment in this world."

"Eradication of I-conceit is indeed the highest happiness."

"One makes oneself lucky; one makes oneself unlucky."

"By oneself is one defiled,
By oneself is one purified,
Both purification and defilement depend on oneself."

"This body is not mine; this am I not; this is not my soul."

"Self-conquest is the best of all conquests."